Reflection Journal:

Life Lessons

Volume I

Dr. Terrie Wurzbacher

This book contains health information of a general nature obtained from scientific and medical sources believed to be accurate. However, this book is not meant to substitute for, and should not be used in place of the health services available from your own health providers.

ISBN-13: 979-8370072741

Independently Published

Cover Credit: Tiberiu Hamunga

Introduction

Welcome to your Reflection Journal. And yes, it is YOUR journal.

If you've read "It's Not About the Miles", you'll know that when I did a "journey run/race" across Tennessee in July 2021, I just "knew" I had to write about that journey's parallels to life. In the 70+ years I've been hanging around, I have learned a great many things - most of them I learned the hard way. After all, I was a red-headed little girl with a typical temperament. I grew up in one of the most competitive communities in the country but was sensitive and shy. I wanted to be a doctor since I was 4 when God proclaimed, "you will be a doctor." So, as you can imagine, I had to develop a thick skin. Making it into and then through medical school was difficult enough but then I served in the US Navy for almost 30 years followed by 16 years working with the Army as a civilian. It was not a career in which you could get away with treading lightly.

I am sure I had impostor syndrome long before there even was an impostor syndrome. Nowhere was this more evident as when I thought I could do this 314 mile race in 10 days totally unsupported. I wanted it something fierce but hadn't made it since I began to try in 2014. In 2014 I didn't finish. In 2015 and 2018 I ended up finishing but with a crew. Even in 2021 I ended up having to have a crew. But I think without the gentleman who crewed me then, I wouldn't have been able to pull this together.

Anyway, in "It's Not About the Miles", I put many life lessons at the end of each section. If you're interested in the whole story, you can read the book. But you don't have to read it to use this journal. I extracted the life lessons from the book and added some questions for you to reflect upon here. You don't have to use my "reflect on" questions. You don't have to actually write in the journal (that's becoming an ancient practice unfortunately - writing helps generate more thought and creativity). You don't have to agree with my life lessons if your experience has led you to different conclusions.

Essentially, you can do what you want with the life lessons. My primary goal is to help you avoid some of the pitfalls I've had to overcome in hopes that you will be wiser than me and hopefully have an easier life.

I hope this enriches your understanding of life, adversity, emotions, and mental discipline!

Terrie Wurzbacher

Let The Journey Begin...

Life Lesson

What's right around the corner might be the best person, place or thing that will ever come into your life. So be courageous and turn that corner. And remember, you must always have something in the wings to work toward when you've reached the summit of your current goal.

Reflect on:

Is there something you feel you "should" do, or want to do but are too afraid or too shy to try?

Write about the "bad" things that could happen if you take the chance. Then write about the good things that could happen.

Now, the harder part... What evidence do you have that any of the "bad" things will happen?

If there isn't solid evidence, ask yourself what's really holding you back. Can you take a tiny brave step to turn that corner?

Try it, just one tiny step...see where it leads you.

Reflections

Life Lesson

All pain is real. The brain creates all pain. The brain doesn't really differentiate between emotional and physical pain. When the brain becomes over-sensitized, often a person will develop chronic pain. This is an epidemic not only in the U.S. but throughout the world. Unfortunately, it's also usually "invisible." I guarantee you know someone with chronic pain, whether you know it. These people are not faking, not embellishing, and the medical community definitely misunderstands them. They are mired in the body of a whale. They are being slowly sucked into suffocating quicksand. You may be next. Examine your life and your lifestyle and research chronic pain. You owe it to your friends and maybe even to yourself.

Reflect on:

List all the medical conditions that you have had in your life. Put an asterisk by the ones that have been chronic (lasted longer than 3 or 4 months). Now put a double asterisk by those that have been associated with some life stressors. Can you see a relationship between the condition and the stress?

If it's too hard to do for yourself, try the same experiment for someone you know well and see if you can see an association between that person's medical conditions and stresses in their lives. Often it is easier to see things like this in others before the light goes on in our own.

Do you think it would be healthy for you to decrease the amount of stress in your life?

If so, what ways can you try to decrease it, no matter how small? Can you start meditating, walking, going to the gym, reading? What helps you relax? Maybe it's just listening to music more. If so, can you schedule a time each day to listen to your favorite tunes?

Reflections

Life Lesson

Mistakes can make or break you. You can learn from them; you can accept them and realize they have and will continue to teach you how to overcome problems. Be happy about the learning experience. OR you can let them ruin everything. You can beat yourself up and call yourself names and have a major pity party. But you know what? That will only bring you down and instead of having a good time and finding ways around the "mistakes," you'll end up down in the dumps and having a totally lousy time. Your self-talk is so important when dealing with errors and mistakes.

Reflect on:

Is there anything in your life that you consider a mistake? For example, was it a mistake for me to wait 30 years before trying to walk across the USA? Most people would think it was. But, on the other side of the coin are several aspects: 1) it was important but not as important as my career of helping people 2) I wasn't as experienced in life and knowing how to deal with people which is important when you're trying to do something like that, 3) the technology is there now and kept me safer and more able to get help.

With that mistake you've identified, can you find a good way to look at it or see something good that came out of it even if you think it was a mistake?

What's going on in your life right now that you can reframe and change your thinking about a "mistake" as a good thing, full of future blessings?

Reflections

Life Lesson

What's right around the corner might be the best person, place or thing that will ever come into your life. So be courageous and turn that corner. And remember, you must always have something in the wings to work toward when you've reached the summit of your current goal.

Reflect on

What is something that you've been avoiding because you were concerned about (afraid of) what you might find and/or how will people think about you?

Make a vow to work on doing this one thing.

Extra, but still important, reflection: What do you have in the wings ready for you to work on when you reach your current goal?

Reflections

Life Lesson

When there is something deep inside you that just has to come out, pay attention. Nurture it and help to birth it for that "something" is part of your soul and is screaming for expression. Do not deny it! For 30 years, I wanted to travel across the USA on foot. I suppressed it due to work and "life". It continued to percolate deep within and when I was 70, it could no longer be denied. I tried it!

Did I succeed? No.

Might I have succeeded had I done it when I was younger? Maybe.

Do I regret it?

No, because regret accomplishes nothing. I am grateful it stayed within, and I could at least try it. I cherish the experience.

Reflect on:

What's the one thing you have deep inside that you've "always wanted to do" but maybe you haven't had the time, finances or couldn't get away from family responsibilities?

Start putting it down on paper now.

Write specifics about what you want and how you will get there.

Make them up if you don't know them yet.

Then visualize yourself in that future time with your goal achieved!

Feel it, feel the excitement, the joy and sense of accomplishment. Visualization is about so much more than just seeing something. "Act as if" you have achieved it

Reflections

Life Lesson

If things don't go as you planned, don't give up hope. The Universe knows better than you do and will deliver the best thing for you - even if you're having difficulty believing that right now.

Reflect on:

Think back through your life and see if you can find instances when you thought something was the worst possible thing that could happen yet when it was all said and done (even if it was years later), you realize it was exactly what needed to happen to make your life better.
When you have at least one of these done, then write/think about your current circumstances, thanking the universe for their presence and declare that you know "Out of this, something good will happen!"

Repeat that frequently along with "Everything Always Works Out for Me!"

Reflections

Life Lesson

Learn that your identity is within, not without. Learn to accept and be yourself, tying no value to what you do or what you've done and accomplished. Know that your identity is within, not without. Learn to accept and be yourself, tying no value to what you do or what you've done and accomplished.

Reflect on:

Are there things that you haven't "succeeded" at and you were so worried about what other people would think OF YOU? There is a difference between what other people think of what happened and what they think of you. Neither of them reflects who you really are, but if you have to worry about something, make it what they think of the situation.

Better yet, focus on what you learned, who you met or saw again. Find bits and pieces of that experience that you enjoyed or even made you happy. It's highly unlikely the ENTIRE event was negative.

Give yourself a challenge to reframe how you think about things for a day - or maybe even just an hour. If that works, continue for another day. And so on. If it doesn't seem to work, examine it and challenge yourself to make it work. Maybe my idea doesn't fit you, but surely you can reframe it.

Reflections

Life Lesson

Just be yourself. You are NOT what you do and not your job; you are YOU with all the outer wear stripped off. There is no shame in standing naked. It's difficult, but it is rewarding. This is similar to the previous lesson, but it should be dealt with separately. For some, this will be more difficult than the last. For others, it will be easier. Are you afraid to retire because you don't know what you'll do with yourself? You don't know how you'll affect anyone again and your life will be a waste? What about your relationships? Are you afraid to change them because of what you will become?

Reflect on:

Look at your job, your family, your friendships... then think what would you be and who would you be if they were all ripped away from you?

Write what you think your values and qualities are. What do you have to offer the world as a plain old human being, not as a lawyer, a CEO, a runner, a doctor, a mother, a caretaker, etc.? That is what you must focus on and cultivate. It's NOT what you DO but what you think, feel and actually are once you tear off the wrapping paper.

Decide if you want to work to cultivate these identified qualities. If you do, start jotting down a plan to implement changes or activities that will help you focus on them more

Reflections

Life Lesson

It's the little things that help people through hard times, whether it's a smile, a nod or a simple "Hi, how are you" You never know what will change the inner turmoil of another person. Two of the most precious things my good friend gave me were insignificant in the grand scheme of life. But they made all the difference to me. One was a small, laminated piece of paper with a QR code on it, so I didn't always have to bring my phone into the gym. How kind that was. And it was a BIG DEAL to me. Another gesture didn't even involve anything material. He listened when I had a decision to make. He asked me questions and then he could give me an opinion that was free of emotion. That was something I couldn't do, and the emotion clouded my judgement.

Reflect on:

Has someone ever done something small or totally unexpected that made you happy? What was it? Thank them! Consider even writing an actual note and sending it via snail mail. They will be surprised.

Next, think of what little things you can do for someone to just bring a bit of happiness. Make a list. Then put them into action.

Reflections

Life Lesson

Keep your eyes and ears open; learn that your "failures" are just feedback. Learn from everything whether it's a success. It's important that you adopt the philosophy that there are no failures. Each alleged failure is really information (feedback) for you to evaluate and make changes. When a baby falls as they try to walk, they don't say "oh well, I'm a failure, I'll never walk so I might as well just crawl all over the place". Heck no. They move to the coffee table or couch and make their way up that personal Mt. Everest and summit when they stand once again. Next comes a simple step. Then another and another and oops, they may fall again. That may seem like a setback and may lead to tears, but after a bit of comfort, they're right back at it. Do you have the tenacity of a baby learning to walk?

Reflect on:

Think of something you considered a failure in your life. Write it down.

Look at what you wrote; hold your hand up by the side of your face; move that hand to the other side across your eyes. Tell yourself as you do that "I wipe away this failure and see only feedback".

Write about what you learned and what you need to do differently next time.

Repeat the process as many times as necessary.

Reflections

Life Lesson

Don't end up regretting what you "never got around to doing." Can you tell how important this concept is? Regret is the last thing you want to have. If you try something and it doesn't work out, at least you won't regret not trying it... always wondering what could have been. Sure, you may need to prioritize some things, but in the long run, it will be well worth it. I know that I would have regretted not trying to walk across the USA if I hadn't tried. It wasn't a success, but I gave it all I had and I have no regrets now. There's no musing "Could I have done it? What would it have been like?"

Reflect on:

Dig deep and list the things you really would like to do.

Prioritize the list.

Most importantly, make plans to do them. They may be vague plans at first, but they are the seeds that you will nurture with your thoughts, writings, and visualizations.

Pick a time to review this list - such as once a month, once a quarter, once a year, etc. The more frequent the better - remember, you're just watering the seeds. You're creating new neural pathways that will let your brain think you're really experiencing it. This will allow your brain to become more comfortable with the idea. The more you do it, the more it will come into existence because you've already seen it in your mind.

Put those frequencies on the calendar. Actually schedule an appointment to do the review and "watering"

Reflections

Life Lesson

Only play the "what if" game when trying to prepare for the unexpected.

It's useless to go back through your life and talk about 'what if". There is no changing the past. You can also do damage if you get to where you are questioning yourself - "what if I don't finish?" - "What if people think I'm too old" - "what if people think I don't belong here?" Playing this "what if" game only serves to send you down the spiral into the abyss. Don't go there. There is so much else you can contemplate.

Reflect on:

When you catch yourself worrying, stop! Instead of "what if?", say "so what?" "Remember to focus only on what you can control, and you certainly cannot control the outcome in most cases. You can control what you put in and that's where you should concentrate.

When thinking about something that happened in the past and notice yourself wondering what might have happened if you did "x" instead of "y", stop! Simply say, "I am on the path I'm supposed to be on even if it doesn't look like it. I am going to make the most of this. I am grateful for this opportunity. This path may lead me to the pot of gold I've been looking for". Edit this to fit your mood and personality but the key is to realize it doesn't MATTER what might have happened. It didn't. Period. Let's move on

Reflections

Life Lesson

Listen to your body...and then do what it tells you. I learned this when my age caught up with me and I was feeling weak, tired, discouraged etc. But it was my body telling me it just needed rest. It had been telling me that for a while, but I let my ego get in the way and ignored it. But, as usual in life, my body won. It's better to listen earlier.

Reflect on:

Find a quiet spot and close your eyes. Can you feel the distinct sensations in your body? You may not initially, but don't give up. Try to find at least one sensation and concentrate on it.

Silently ask it what it's trying to tell you.

Be quiet for a few minutes and listen for an answer. Don't create one. Just let it come. And if there is no answer, don't give up on it. It will take time. Keep practicing. Maybe try it when you're in bed if you don't fall asleep right away. Or maybe in the morning if it's quiet then.

Write the stresses in your life right now. What's going on? Do you feel overwhelmed? Do you feel stressed (that is a personal thing)?

Is there anything you can do about at least one of those stresses?

Note: Consider looking at "Whole Brain Living" by Dr. Jill Bolte Taylor

Reflections

Life Lesson

Process over outcome. You can control the process, or what you put into the process. You cannot control the outcome. If you know the steps for doing something (and the smaller you break them down, the better), it's up to you to determine how much effort you're going to put into it. Focus on being and doing better, not on what you want to happen or what might happen.

Of course, you have a goal, but imagining that goal and researching/analyzing it carefully is what got you to the specific process. Whether you do those individual steps today is all you can control. Be in the present. You can't determine what the result will be. For example, I started a mental toughness challenge to cut out the foods that I am addicted to (ice cream primarily but also chips) and on the third day I was so proud of myself... UNTIL... I stepped on that darn piece of metal that rules our lives so often (the scale). I had gained 3 pounds from the last time I had weighed. For the first time in my life, though, I didn't allow that "fact" (it's really just a number) to be my excuse to say, "It didn't work, I quit". I realized that what I was really after was strengthening my mental discipline. That was going to take time. So what if today's "number" was funky? I got back to understanding and pursuing the process. Since that time, I haven't weighed myself. I can't control what the scale says, but I can control what I put in my mouth.

Reflect on:

When your goal is not immediate and will take a bit of time, make a sign that says, "process over outcome" and stick it where you need it. If you're trying to take off weight, put it over the number on the scale or right near it.

Repeat "it's the process that matters right now! The outcome will take care of itself."

Reflections

Life Lesson

Behind every physical challenge is a mental challenge. It does very little good to work on your body and physical strength without also striving to become the strongest you can be mentally. Not everyone's mental obstacles are the same, even though a particular physical event might have the same components for everyone. Look inside–deep inside–and determine where your weaknesses are. Then you try to figure out what is behind them at the same time as you research ways to overcome those mental barriers. Internal examination is the key to building strong mental resilience so that your physical prowess can do what you want it to do.

Reflect on:

Pick something that is a challenge for you right now.

Look deep inside and see what are your areas of weakness: Do you worry too much and never figure out what action to take? Are you pessimistic about everything that seems "bad"?

Write these things down.

Try to determine why you act these ways. Is it just "the way it's always been"? Has it become a habit?

If it is just a habit, you can change it.

Is this a way to help you feel as if you're in control? If so, do you really think you can control the outcome?

Vow to really evaluate what you're thinking and see if you can try another way.

Reflections

Life Lesson

You hear this all the time, but it's true. Preparation is an essential ingredient for success. I "knew it" but didn't really comprehend it until this year when I saw how much the year of preparation contributed to my feeling I could do it and be successful. And when I achieved my goal, I was convinced. You need to prepare in all ways for any aspect of life–physically, mentally, and emotionally. There is a thing called "adaptive stress" and that is the stress you experience that helps build your muscles, whether they be physical muscles, mental ones or emotional ones. When you're afraid of something, you can overcome it by repeated exposure, starting with exposure in your mind while you are in a safe environment and preferably with supportive people around you.

You gain experience as you go through any event in your life and from this experience, you can learn the preparation necessary for you to handle similar occurrences better. How can you vary your training (for every aspect of your life) to improve your outcome?

Reflect on:

Look back to something you've done before and analyze how much you prepared.

Were you happy with the results?

If so, you may not need much tweaking.

If you're not happy, though, what could you do to prepare differently?

How can you apply this thinking about a past event to something going on in your life right now?

Reflections

Life Lesson

We all have fears. One of the first things to do if you want to overcome these fears is to be aware of what they are. Awareness, interestingly, is the key to understanding what we need to do to change ANYTHING. Once you've identified these issues, prioritize them. Don't set yourself up for failure by trying to conquer them all. You can either pick the most important or, perhaps, you want to go slow, and you can pick the thing you're least afraid of. It's up to you. It's all about choice. Once you've listed them all, you can see if any overlap and hopefully, you'll also be able to see what has held you back. Until that point, you might just think that you "can't do it" and don't even understand why. Wouldn't it be nice if you found out it was just one thing and that with the appropriate coaching and approach, you could overcome that? Then you could move on with your life. Besides the list, it would help if you could identify some person or people that you trust to help you confront this fear.

Reflect on:

Write your fears. This may take a while because I want you to look at your deepest level, not just the superficial ones like "spiders". Writing them out is your first step toward awareness. Awareness is necessary before change.

Pick one fear. Right down situations you can use to invoke some minor change. The key is making it minor. Ask yourself if there's anything deeper. Why are you afraid of "x"? What do you think will happen if "x" occurs? Is there evidence that this will or has happened before? If so, is it still likely to happen, or has enough time passed that it probably won't occur again? If there is no evidence, how do you feel about that?

Come up with one thing you can do to conquer a tiny piece of this fear. When you do, celebrate!

Then repeat with another piece.

Reflections

Life Lesson

Get yourself some mantras. We've talked about that in other places. They will help you combat that voice in your head that wants to tell you how bad you are or how stupid it is to keep trying. Think of the one or two that you choose as "turning up the volume" to drown out that voice–and replace it with something that is positive and meaningful to you. I've given you examples that really work for me. But here are some others:

- Be the victor, not the victim

- Passion conquers pain (this applies to all types of pain – physical and emotional)

-"Bring it on". Show your brain, you're not afraid and it shouldn't be either. You look forward to anything the universe wants to give you as a challenge and a growth process.

-When it gets harder, I get stronger and enjoy it more.

Reflect on:

Pick one of these mantras or come up with your own. It must be something you'll easily remember and be able to repeat whenever you need it.

Practice saying it to yourself repeatedly until it becomes automatic. Keep at it.

Reflections

Life Lesson

Acting changes everything. It's been proven that if you act a certain way, your emotions will follow. So, if you stand up straight instead of being stooped over, hold your head up high and smile, you're more likely to feel more confident and happier. Try it.

Reflect on:

Practice (in front of a mirror is always helpful) being in different body positions and see how you feel.

When you're in the middle of an activity (workout, race, meeting, standing in line), change your posture to a more confident stance and note how it changes things inside you.

Reflections

Life Lesson

Keep journals! This is not for sissies who have to write "In their diaries"–ha–far from it. Athletes call them training logs. I still have mine from the first several years I was running and especially when I was training for a marathon. But, given any life event, you can benefit from recording your thoughts and feelings and metrics if they are available (obviously there are many things in life that don't have specific measurements but there is always something you can use to see if you're progressing or regressing).

Let's take the example of being irritable again. If you record your daily activities, including how much sleep you got and the quality of that sleep, then you may correlate less sleep with your mood. That way, you may see a pattern and when you do, you can change it. If you don't look, you probably won't see a pattern and then you're subject to what I call an "unknown force".

I use an app on my phone called Moment Diary and I just record some basics every day and then other things that happen. I also have a training journal (training log) where I record my events and progress so I can see what I need to do more of, for example. I also have a regular journal where I will write about my feelings and my parts (from IFS/Internal Family Systems).

Reflect on:

What behaviors would you like to track?

What metrics could you use to track the improvements in those behaviors?

What tools do you already have that could help you track your proress?

Reflections

Life Lesson

Many successful people have a start, stop, continue process they use every day. They write about what happened that day that they would like to start. For instance, someone wants to get more quiet time before their family gets up. They may put under start something like "get up 15 minutes earlier".

Next up is something that if you stopped it, things might be better. Example: "I will stop playing games on my computer at least an hour before bed".

Last in this short list is what do I want to continue since it seems to be "working". Example: "I want to continue spending time with my son, helping him with his homework or just talking about his day. This seems to give us quality time since we've scheduled it and keep to it. It's helped us both."

You should also record things you overcame and how. You can reference this at a future time when a similar situation presents itself.

It's also helpful to do a weekly and monthly summary—you pick what you want to track (e.g., you're eating foods you don't really want to, how many times you stayed up too late and what happened, how well you did on your hydration plan, how many times you made it to the gym, etc). Again, you can't really change what you don't measure.

Believe me, when you get older (maybe a lot or a little older), you'll be grateful you did.

Reflect on:

Are you willing to try all the above? If so, get at least one or maybe more paper journals if that suits you. If you're totally tech, use any of many computer apps. Make a vow to record whatever it is you want to track for at least a month. Determine how often you will record things - every day; just after workouts or races; once a week, etc.

Reflections

Life Lesson

Celebrate your successes—even if it's just with yourself. I had two big successes doing a 37 day mental toughness challenge. We started the day after Thanksgiving and by doing it every day for 37 days, your new year's resolutions will be habits by then. Anyway, by looking at this challenge of not eating certain foods to build more resilience and mental toughness, I got out of the "deprivation" thinking pattern. And I also could focus on "process over outcome" without worrying when the first weight I had after I started the challenge showed an increase. In the past, I would have just given up. But it was about so much more than the number on the scale. It was about being able to be in control of my urges/addictions. There was another time I overcame the inner talk that wanted me to break the discipline, and I was able for the first time to conquer that voice. I was ecstatic and not only recorded it in my daily journal but wrote to Dr. Gilbert of Success Hot Line, who created this way of framing things and to whom I owe so much more of my success.

Reflect on:

No matter how small you may think it is, record your successes in some form - electronic or paper. But make them retrievable so you can look at them again when things may not be going the way you'd like.

Reflections

Life Lesson

Learn from your obstacles. Instead of just sticking your head in the sand and being happy they are gone, analyze them. Were they as big as you feared? Maybe even bigger? How did you approach them? Were you able to keep your emotions out of the picture or did your negative or positive thinking habit get in the way? Were they preventable? What can you do differently next time, if anything? What did you learn?

Reflect on:

What obstacles are you facing right now? If you're doing ok now, look at some that have appeared in the past.

What were they all about?

What emotions are in the way of looking at them objectively (anger, fear, etc.)?

Can you break them down into feasible solutions?

Who can you ask for help with them?

Try your best to remove the emotional component when trying to problem solve.

Reflections

Life Lesson

Anticipate obstacles/adversity whenever you can. As you get ready for some event (race, wedding, vacation, surgical procedure, or treatment), see if you can write about some potential obstacles. If you can, then research solutions. I'll give you a great example. One of my friends had breast cancer with surgery and chemotherapy. There were so many things that she couldn't do without a lot of help, so she wrote a book about what to expect and how to handle them. These were obstacles no one ever talks about, such as how to get out of a chair when you can't use your arms because of surgery or drains or whatever. When to get worried about some symptoms they don't advise you about. People who give these treatments usually haven't had them and don't know what you will have problems with. You can find out how to do so many things on the internet and they may even tell you some of what you can expect–let's say you're going to Yellowstone National Park on vacation. I bet if you searched for something like "potential problems vacationing at Yellowstone", you'd find info. You can also search social media for both obstacles and solutions. Everyone on social media wants to "help" you with their advice. Just be careful what you believe. Do your research. Remember what we talked about earlier– "OMMS" Obstacles Make Me Stronger (thanks to Brian Johnson). And you can build that strength by trying to expect some of them.

Reflect on:

What things have been obstacles for you in the past (e.g., fear)?

Do you expect those things to be present again?

What can you do to mitigate them and come up with an alternative plan?

Remember OMMS - Obstacles Make Me Stronger

Reflections

Life Lesson

Again, another no-brainer. If you keep doing the same thing over and over, you're most likely going to get the same results. Some of that is because we are such creatures of habit, but another part is our significant resistance to change. We don't even want to change when we SEE that "our way" hasn't produced what we want. Often, it's easier (although much less effective) to blame something (or someone) else for the lack of success. It's hard to look at yourself and say "uh, OK, so this way hasn't been working. What can I do differently? Who do I know that can help me figure out a better way? Where can I get help with this? I know it will be hard, but I feel it would be worth it."

That last part is key. Take weight loss, for example. It's so easy to say "well, that diet doesn't work." Instead, we have to look at what we're really putting in our bodies and how long have we been trying it. Sometimes, our desire for instant gratification impedes basic reason. I speak from experience because I would always try to find something "out there" that I could say was the reason I couldn't lose weight. But, if you're not too far gone in whatever endeavor you're engaging in, figure out what you need to do to make it work. Then, you have to do the work. It's not good enough to just figure it out.

Reflect on:

What things do you do over and over and are you happy with the results of doing those things (e.g. do you always screw up your diet because you just can't resist the ice cream in the freezer?).

What can you do differently to prevent that from happening (e.g., don't keep ice cream in the house? If it's a family thing, ask them to help you by not having it in the house - explain you need their help)?

Reflections

Life Lesson

A corollary to making a change, is to give whatever process you pick long enough to work before you discard it. We want things to work overnight, and that's just not going to happen. This is where you can concentrate on "process over outcome". That will help you focus on the present moment and not on the results. When you follow the process you just have to trust in it to work and not just give up because what I want to happen didn't happen overnight."

Reflect on:

Before you start on a project or goal, what can you stop doing so that you get different results?

How long do you think you should allow before judging the outcome as a success or failure?

Does it have to be a success or failure? Could you measure it on a scale so that even a small bit of progress would be considered progress? What scale might you use?

Reflections

Life Lesson

Sometimes you must do things on your own. I learned this the hard way. In all my other attempts at Vol State (the 314 mile race across Tennessee) I had followed others and thought I had to do things the way they did. If they stayed at a motel, I thought I had to as well. If they stopped frequently, I thought I should too. But I didn't know that each person has to run their own race–whether that's on the road or in life. I had more trouble with meeting the cutoffs when I did what others did–without figuring out if that would work for me; without analyzing it. Much of that was from a lack of self-confidence, so I didn't think I had any business thinking for myself. It was also because of fear–fear of trying something different, of being different. I missed out on so much in my life because of that insecurity and fear. Do NOT let it happen to you.

Reflect on:

Are there any times in your life when you thought you should just follow someone else and do what they do?

If so, how did that work out?

If it worked out well, is there anything you can do to make it even better? Maybe not.

If things didn't work as you'd like them, what can you do differently (e.g., in my race across Tennessee, I stopped waiting at stores or angel stops until the other folks left. I stayed for what I thought was the appropriate time for me to rest, recoup, and yet not get behind. That was different for me than for others. Only I could make that determination.)

You have to be your own boss.

Reflections

Life Lesson

Awareness is the key to everything. Get yourself off the emotional roller coaster (and better yet, don't get on it in the first place). It will take you nowhere but into the abyss of despair... and you'll get motion sick on the way. Learn to accept your emotions but stop there. Do NOT let them control your responses or your actions. Especially anger. No one thinks clearly when angry. The frontal lobe loses a major amount of blood supply when you get angry. Don't make any decisions when you're angry (or hungry or tired). They will be the ones you regret. You use too much energy being angry and it depletes the amount you have to do the things you need to do to succeed.

Reflect on:

Can you think of times when you've let your emotions get the best of you?

What are your triggers? It takes an aware person to admit that something triggers them.

Once you can identify them, though, you can plan in advance if there's some other response (vice a reaction) that you'd like to substitute.

Perhaps there's certain situations in traffic that get you angry, such as a red light.

What can you do to take down the anger a bit?

Is there a song you can sing, a mantra you can say?

Once you come up with something, make sure you repeat it often, so it becomes fixed in your brain

Reflections

Life Lesson

If you're going to convince yourself of something, make it something positive. I was convinced I couldn't finish the 314 mile race in time unsupported. So, guess what? I didn't. Until the year someone kicked me in the butt and told me I was ahead of the cutoffs consistently and there was no reason I couldn't do this unsupported. For some reason, when she said that, things that had been scattered in my soul for all these years came together and clicked together like Lego toys. There are all the pieces you need deep in your soul, too. Don't let them remain dormant for as long as I did. Find them and cultivate them. Don't listen to anyone who ever says YOU can't do something. What they mean is that they can't, so they don't want you to even try. Of course, you have to do your research and find out what it takes. But if you want something bad enough, you will find a way to do it. Surround yourself with people who have also done seemingly impossible things. They will help you get there!

Reflect on:

What are you "convinced" of? Is it something positive or negative?

If it's not positive, what can you do to change that opinion because that's all it is - an opinion? Force yourself to show your brain the evidence that this will be true.

You probably don't have that evidence. I have a "part" that I call the Fact Checker. When some other "naysayer part" starts yapping, telling me I can't do x, y, or z or that something bad will happen, I ask that part what evidence he or she has. Then, I turn to the Fact Checker to ask for her evidence - whether it's proof positive or proof negative she will show me the proof - e.g., "there have been 10 out 11 times that this positive thing happened when these circumstances occur". This shuts up the "naysayer" quickly.

Reflections

Life Lesson

Keep in the present moment. My constant mental companion was "W.I.N" - what's important now? It was always "just keep moving" or "just get to the next section" - never more. In fact, when I got to the deepest part of the abyss, I had gotten away from the present moment. But I was able to bring myself back. I also dealt frequently with "control the controllables." I couldn't do anything about the heat or the weather or the hills. All I could do was make sure I was hydrating and had enough fluids and keep going. The rest would just happen. This took away a lot of mental anguish and kept me going. I also used "I can do this" and "this, too, shall pass". In the second to last mile, the uncertainty of that totally dark road almost sucked under me. Even though my lamps helped me see what was under my feet, the not knowing what was surrounding me got to me and I was getting upset that "it would never end". Then I realized it was just me not knowing what was or wasn't there—the simple not knowing. I finally knew that it wasn't anything bad or anything to even be concerned with. I could let go of having to control all that was around me, and that was huge. It let me calmly keep on going and guess what, the end of that road came rapidly after that.

Reflect on:

When things to be spiraling out of control, can you try to stop the chaos inside your skull by asking "What's Important Now"? Do not allow yourself to go beyond "now". Just keep saying W.I.N.

Reflections

Life Lesson

Never underestimate how much a simple act of kindness will mean. I will never forget BJ nor what he did for me. This little dime signifies love and concern and a wonderful beating heart of a human being. On the day of the bus ride to the start line, he gave me a dime to carry with me. It is the lightest coin, and they made this one in 1947 so it was a year older than me. I made it into a necklace so I can carry BJ and his support with me all the time. Open your eyes and your heart and something similar will happen to you. On my first attempt when I knew nothing, I was walking along this lonely road when a lady stopped and asked if I wanted a bottle of water. It was like manna from heaven. She gave me the water and an apple and then drove away. I felt really blessed, but didn't realize how very blessed I was. She has become a fantastic friend ever since. Accept everything and know that there is a blessing behind it. You just have to relax and let the curtain fall away.

Reflect on:

Is there something you can do for someone that shows you love and care for them?

Is there something that someone has done for you that will stay with you forever? If so, shout it from the rooftop - or make sure people know about it and who gave it to you. We should use social media for more good and this is one way

Reflections

Life Lesson

God (or whatever higher power you believe in. I prefer to call it the Universe) always knows what's best for you. Much to your dismay, you do not know what's best for you. Everywhere you turn, you find people telling you that despite the pain some horrible thing (or maybe just unfortunate, not rising to the level of 'horrible') caused in their life, something better came out of it. Fights with your spouse/family/significant other/best friend can lead to a much better understanding and ultimately acceptance of each other. Illnesses and injuries can lead to discovery of other aspects of life that you may not have had time for. This has been the case in my life and I could write a book about it. I'll just give you one example..

I absolutely hated running and was very glad I was in the Navy because a swim test was permitted in place of running for our physical fitness test. In 1993, I tore my ACL and had it surgically repaired. 6 months later, I decided I needed to see if could run so that I could play softball (I played catcher and had to run to cover first base). I was so fat, out of shape and smoked 3-4 packs of cigarettes a day, it wasn't a pretty sight. I vowed to practice until I could run to the end of the block (0.35 mile) without stopping. By the time I could do that (one week), I was hooked on running. Without running, I do not know how sad my life would have been. Running and the relationships I've made because of it, has enriched my life in ways I can't express.

Reflect on:

No matter what has gone "wrong", declare it good and say, "out of this something good will happen". Say it until you're blue in the face - it doesn't matter if you don't totally believe it (although you should, especially if you objectively look back at your life).

Reflections

Life Lesson

Be open to strange things and strange people. A synonym for "strange" here could also be "different". Often, we will reject situations and people immediately just because they don't do things the way we do or don't think as we do. I've recently had this experience but had a life-changing encounter when I was young. It's made me take my pickaxe to that brick wall, resisting change and opening a way that I can embrace others no matter what. When I had been rejected at medical school, I had to get a job and ended up in a Catholic hospital as a lab person (just a 'person', not even a 'tech'). I am not Catholic. Because I had been rejected, I had lost faith in God. After all, God told me when I was 4 that I was going to be a doctor. And now he had let me down (little did I know that was another 'best thing that ever happened'). Anyway, the nun who was my supervisor was the most amazing patient person I've ever met. She answered all my questions about God, but not in the usual stereotypical way that many religious figures (and sometimes parents) do. She also helped me when I was diagnosed with epilepsy and couldn't drive for three weeks while the medication kicked in. One time while working for the Army, there was a significant change in the leadership style and personnel. It was "different", but I opened my heart and my mind (often it takes both) to see what they had to say, and the changes turned out to be the right ones, even if they were different.

Reflect on:

Whenever you think someone is "strange" or has done something "weird", stop and ask yourself how they (or it) differ from you.

Is something making you uncomfortable? How are you defining "strange" or "weird"?

Is it because it's not the way you're used to doing things? What if you looked at it as just another way of being or doing?

Reflections

Life Lesson

Gratitude can turn a negative into a positive. Find a way to be thankful for your troubles, and they can become your blessings. Say something like "everything always works out for me", or "out of this something good will happen." Say it, even if you don't believe it. If you repeat it enough, you will begin to believe it. The energy you put out will then be positive and will bring more positive into your life. Death is often the one situation people can't explain. If you can look at the results of a loved one's death objectively, you see that you have changed and grown because of the experience. Not that you won't miss that person or that you shouldn't grieve or feel bad. Just express the gratitude for that person's life and all the good he/she brought into yours. Open yourself to receive the blessing of this painful time.

Reflect on:

Start a gratitude practice. Do it every day.

There are a million ways to do this. Look them up or simply find a notebook or something on your computer and record three things you're grateful for every day. If it's a cruddy day, you can still be thankful for being alive, for the roads to travel on, for having enough money to have bought this book, anything. You can even be grateful for the problems that made the day cruddy.

The more you are thankful for them, the more they will turn out well.

Reflections

Life Lesson

The only thing that's constant in our universe is change. I always resisted hearing this, but now I understand it and embrace it. If we recognize that, then each day we can examine our lives differently and see the benefits. We are always changing. Let us grow as we change.

Reflect on:

Embrace change.

Whenever things are going to change or have changed, shout out (even if it's in your head) "Thank you". Change is good.

Finish this sentence: "If _____ hadn't changed, I wouldn't have _____"

Do this every day or make one long list and then, when something else is about to change, say, "I am happy about this change because I know something good will happen from it."

Reflections

Life Lesson

It's the start that stops people. I learned this from Dr. Robert Gilbert and Brian Cain–both mental conditioning experts. Once you overcome the inertia (aka comfort zone) and begin something, continuing it is a whole lot easier. Look at the boulder at the top of the hill. Getting that heavy piece of rock to move takes a tremendous effort. Once it's going, though, it's so much easier to keep it moving. Take that first step. Don't even think about what's tomorrow or later today. Focus on what you need to do RIGHT NOW to get started on what you want to achieve. Use the 15 minute rule people are always advocating. Start doing something but tell yourself you only have to do it for 15 minutes. Once the 15 minutes is over, you can do something else. Or you can continue doing what you started. When I finally decluttered my house during the pandemic, I set my timer for 15 minutes, telling myself that was all I had to do. Two things shocked me: 1) How much I got done in 15 minutes and 2) I always continued well past the 15 minutes. And then I was eager to do it again the next day.

Reflect on:

What is one thing you want to get started on but "never get to"? Write it down.

What's one small step you can take to actually start? Then do the 15-minute test I described above. Set your timer. When you're finished with the experiment, write how you felt.

Repeat it tomorrow.

Then the next day, but don't think of all those days, just think of right now.

Reflections

Life Lesson

Always remember how Mohammed Ali hated training: "I hated every minute of training, but I said, 'Don't quit. Suffer now and live the rest of your life as a champion.'" You have already come up with your "Why", hopefully. Now, you only have to remember that why and know that everything you are doing will take you closer to it. Put your maximum effort into every attempt (workout, conversation, etc.). Make every one count. I know what it's like to go to the gym and just go through the motions. You just want to "check the box" that you did it. But ask yourself, what did you get out of that time? Did you put your "all" into it? If not, did you really get any closer to your "why"? If you have an accountability partner that can hold your toes to the fire, great. But, if not, you have to do it yourself. Remember the keywords–present moment. Do and Be your best every moment.

Reflect on:

What is it you want to achieve with all the training you have to do?

Just remember what Mohammed Ali kept telling himself.

Repeat this or your own saying until it clicks.

Reflections

Life Lesson

No matter what you're after in life, determine the destination and then take a lot of time figuring out the tiny steps that need to be taken every day to reach that destination. That is the backbone of achieving any goal. It's not enough to just set the goal. Plan to achieve it too. That involves breaking it down into much smaller parts. A child might want to build a skyscraper out of his LEGO toys and he can envision the result. However, that same child has to know how to start and you start with the basic foundation, not as sexy as the finished product, but vital to its overall success. The skyscraper cannot materialize without the foundation

Reflect on:

Take the goals (or even just the projects) you have going for you. Start making a list of the different components.

Go back over this list several times and break each step you initially wrote into smaller steps until you have a comprehensive list.

You can pick which steps you want to achieve when. "By Wednesday, I should be able to get steps 1-3 done; after that, I'll do step 4 several more times, etc."

Once you see them all listed, you'll know how to view them in your mind's eye.

.

Reflections

Life Lesson

Learn to "chunk". Chunk everything down into pieces. There are different ways to chunk. You can create fairly large chunks, but it always works better if you create the smallest chunks possible. This technique helps you not to be overwhelmed and stalled. Or, worse yet, quit. If I had only focused on having to cover 314 miles, I would have become overwhelmed rather quickly and would not have had any reserve energy to keep going. But when I broke it down first into having to do 31.4 miles each day and then even further into 15.7 miles every 12 hours, it made it much more conceivable and therefore more "doable". Frequently, I had to break it down even further into "just another mile" or even "I know I can make it to that guardrail". The entire purpose is to give yourself something to keep going for that you know you can reach.

Reflect on:

It may be something simple as my mile at a time example. Or it may be more complex.

The point is to create these "bite-sized" chunks on a regular basis – almost automatically when you face a new challenge.

Reflections

Life Lesson

The road's shoulders parallel the road of life. What's on your shoulders? Can you open them wide to all those who are in your path and who could benefit from your touch? That's what we are here for - not to hold ourselves closed but to open up and let people in. So many people are in need, but you'd never know it by looking at them. Let them all in and you'll save more than you realize.

Reflect on:

How wide are your shoulders?

Can you overcome a "scarcity" mentality by widening your shoulders into a "prosperity" mode?

Do you know someone who might need to bum a ride on your shoulders?

What can you do to help?

Reflections

Life Lesson

Distractions or other diversions help to keep your mind off things you are worrying about. You know the worry doesn't do any good, but it's hard to just say "let go". That's why you do yourself a service by focusing on something else. Before you know it, the stress and fear chemicals will metabolize out of your system, and you can view the situation more objectively.

Reflect on:

What distractions are in your life?

How are they affecting you and your quality of life?

What can you do about them? Can you let go or maybe find a different one to substitute (come up with a mantra that will get you back on track)?

Who can you ask for help to minimize your distractions?

Reflections

Life Lesson

Once you know your starting point and your destination, concentrate on making it the next 200 feet and then repeat. You can get anywhere if you go about it correctly. Have courage to take steps into the darkness if you want something enough.

Reflect on:

Repeat "200 feet" whenever you feel you don't know how to get to your goal.

You can always make it another 200 feet and then reassess.

Just keep going.

Reflections

Life Lesson

The year (or years) is a chain-link fence and to keep the links in line, we have to address each section. No matter how good your memory is, you won't be able to remember in September what you said you were going to do or even what you did in February. Write it down.

If you take 5 minutes at the same time each day, those 5 minutes will give you focus to guide your actions and decisions this month.

Reflect on:

Review each month as it ends. Decide what progress you've made.

Use the stop, start, and continue process we talk about elsewhere.

What do you want to stop so you can make better progress (e.g., eating after a certain hour at night)?

What do you want to start doing to improve your progress (e.g., reading 20 pages every day)?

What do you want to continue because you see that it's working (e.g., going to bed at a set time every night)?

Here are the questions to ask:

- How can I make the most of this month?

- What's my goal(s) for this month?

- What do I need to continue to have a better chance of reaching my goal?

- What do I need to work on to ensure I reach this month's goal?

Reflections

Life Lesson

Take some time and write in a notebook, recording as many past accomplishments as possible that you can think of. Call it your "confidence journal" or "confidence resume". You can draw from this whenever you're thinking things may be beyond you. This works to bolster your spirits and helps you solve problems when you realize you've come across something like this before. Take some photos of it and carry them with you on your journey. When you're feeling like you just don't have it in you, look at your accomplishments and draw confidence and good feelings from that list. You can even envision having conquered this current adversity and adding it to your list. Keep reading and using your mantra until your energy level has improved. Looking at your past accomplishments hopefully will show that you have more strength than you think you do right now.

Reflect on:

Spend time each day creating your confidence resume.

Read it frequently

Reflections

Life Lesson

Plan and prepare for the unexpected. It's hard to know how to prepare for the unexpected. You can't normally figure out all the variables that might happen. But you should know that your plan may totally go out the door and instead of reacting with a deer in the headlights pose, you'll be ready to adapt. It always helps to practice some of that adaptation as often as you can. When you gather the info above, you'll see what other people have endured and that will give you thoughts. For example, one racer in the recent HOTS race had a broken pack and had to figure out how to carry all the gear the rest of the way. That gave me something to think about. Not to panic about it, but to plan a "what if" situation.

Reflect on:

For this exercise, it's appropriate to come up with a list of "what-ifs".

But it's required that you go further than just making the list. List the ways you'll be able to change your plans to fit those situations. Include everything you can think of on both lists.

Reflections

Life Lesson

You always have the choice to say, "I choose to feel good."

This sounds really stupid, but I have worked with it and it helps. Especially if you head down "Worry Lane". If you think about "I feel so tired or sick or whatever", start saying to yourself "I choose to feel good." You know what they say - "Pain is inevitable, suffering is optional".

Reflect on:

Add "I choose to feel good" to your vocabulary. Try to use it at least once every day.

Change your language, too, to switch "I get to" instead of "I have to"

Reflections

Life Lesson

Enjoy the journey. Don't wait for the end.

*You learn so much each day. You wake up as a different person
each day. Think about how you've changed since day 1 in your
training (or in this phase of your life). When you wake up every
morning, say "hi" to the new you. What have you experienced as
you've come along on this training event (or phase/project)?. If
you don't pay attention, don't enjoy and don't learn from each
day, your heartbreak will be worse if you don't achieve your
ultimate "goal".*

Reflect on:

Is there anything interfering with you enjoying your journey?

*Every day (morning or night) ask yourself "HOW have I
changed in the past 24 hours".*

Don't ask "have I changed?"

*We all change constantly. Every interaction with another person
creates some sort of change in each person.*

Just be aware of it and celebrate this.

Reflections

Life Lesson

Define your own "success" and "failure".

Success and failure are individual. For me, one success is that I've done really well in training. Another will be when I get to the start, and then there will be many more along the way. I no longer really think of something as a failure, but more I think of it as what have I learned. That doesn't mean I won't be disappointed if I don't finish, but that's not the same as declaring myself a failure. As the great Dr. Robert Gilbert says, "there is no failure, only feedback." Sure, the result may sting for a while, and you are allowed to feel down for a short time. But, put a limit on it and when that limit is up, move on and determine what the feedback was.

Reflect on:

What is on your plate right now?

Define success for each - for you, not based on other's definitions

Define failure in the same way. Then look at this definition and change it into feedback ("ok, this didn't go as planned. What did I learn from it?"

Do these definitions for everything that comes up in your life and refer to them frequently.

Reflections

Life Lesson

Be there for others. This should need no explanation. If you reach out to help others along the way, you'll be doing more good than you can imagine. There are so many ways you can be there for someone else. Even just smiling and saying "hi" can save a life. You never know who needs a friendly face and voice— so, what do you have to lose by smiling and offering a sincere greeting? Think of a time when you've been "down" or things haven't been going the way you'd like and someone smiled at you and said "good morning! How are you?". I imagine that got your "feel good" juices going. It's going to make you feel good too, so don't do it only for others but for yourself too.

Reflect on:

How can you apply this principle in your daily life for at least the next week?

What were your results when you've done this in the past?

Reflections

Life Lesson

Know where others are coming from and don't let them, or their chatter intimidate you. This is kind of a corollary of the "don't play the comparison game" but stay within yourself. Others may put on a brave front and bravado, but you have no clue what's going on inside of them - and what difference does it make, anyway? What matters is where you are in yourself.

Reflect on:

Do you find yourself thinking how much better people are and you don't have any business trying to do something?

How well do you know that person?

Are they really that much better than you?

So what?

What do you want to do?

Do it and to heck with the others!

Reflections

Life Lesson

When things suck, don't give up. Know that they will change. It's not permanent. This is where you need to remember that the only thing that's consistent is change! This is something that's important to remember not only in a race, but in life. No matter how bad things may seem right now, they will change and most likely for the better. You may be tired or hurting, but you just need to keep putting one foot in front of the other, knowing that eventually you will feel different. You just have to keep it forefront of my life. It is possible to allow yourself a 5 minute pity party. Then move on.

Reflect on:

What is in your life right now that seems like it's a dead end?

What can you do to keep yourself going?

Maybe it's W.I.N (What's Important Now) or the "200 feet" concept.

Find something to aim for. Often when running and out of energy, you just shoot for the next telephone pole (I'm particularly fond of guardrails, so that's what I want to reach when they are on this road. If there're no guardrails, I'll pick something that is such as a tree or sign or anything that's just a bit ahead).

Reflections

Life Lesson

The world won't end if you don't "win". First, decide what "win" means - this is like success and failure. But more importantly, put everything into perspective. As I kept saying when I hurt my knee, it's nothing in the grand scheme of things - especially with all the death, illness and disaster people have endured and are still enduring in so many places.

Reflect on:

List situations going on in your life right now.

Next, put down what you would consider a "win" in each situation.

Reflections

Life Lesson

Know who to listen to and who to ask for advice. We are not in life alone and in preparation for upcoming events, ask for help but ask people who have the experience. For example, if I could go back to my childhood era and I was doing this event, I would seek advice from my grandfather who was a mail carrier and walked God knows how many miles every day, carrying a pack that weighed even more than my pack. He would have had brilliant advice, I'm sure.

Reflect on:

List all the people you know you can rely on and for what.

Start asking for advice - especially from those who are older and may not be around much longer. Their wisdom will be lost forever.

Reflections

Life Lesson

Emotions serve a grand purpose in life, but they should not rule your life. Sometimes you have to learn to compartmentalize them and simply leave them in your grocery cart as you proceed down the aisles of life. Ask yourself if the emotions you're feeling right now are serving any useful purpose. If not, what can you do about it? Practice and start with minor things like annoyances and frustrations. This should start building your compartmentalization muscles. Remember to focus on those things you can control.

Reflect on:

Keep a list of things that are going on inside you now. E.g., You need something inspected in your home and they can't give you anything more definite than "you have to be home from 8 to 4".

This really messes up your schedule.

What emotions are you feeling right now?

How do these emotions make you feel about the situation? Do they seem to make things worse or better?

If they are making it worse, do you have to deal with them or can you just let them go? Pretend they are pieces of confetti that you toss into the air to float down onto the streets of a big city where they will never be noticed. Come up with your own visual that will help you a) acknowledge them, but then b) let them go so you can move on with positive things.

Reflections

Life Lesson

When you judge someone negatively, step back and realize that you're doing it. Ask yourself if you would like that person to be doing the same to you and not giving you any benefit of the doubt. If the answer is no, then instead of judging negatively, switch your "dial" to the positive side and force yourself to find at least one good thing about that person. Make this a habit and you'll change. Awareness of what you're doing is the first step to change. Remember that everyone has some good in them. It's our job to expose it to the world!

Reflect on:

Next time you judge someone negatively, ask the above question.

Why do you think you're taking the time to make a judgment?

Is it something you wish you had or were?

If so, how badly do you wish you had it or were it?

If you want it so very much, then add it to your goal list and start using that person or situation to add steps to your "achieving my goal list". It's all about reframing.

Reflections

Life Lesson

If you want something enough, focus all your attention on it and you'll get there. You have to do the work, but such focus will program your subconscious to help you achieve it. Here's my best example:

I spent a year (July 2021 to July 2022) living, breathing and thinking Vol State (the 314 mile journey run across Tennessee in July). So many things didn't click in 2021 and as I started writing my book about it ("It's Not About the Miles") I realized I had beaten myself in so many ways. As a result, my first task was to study and learn mental discipline. Writing the book brought the race foremost to my mind almost every single day. I delved deep into what went wrong and then spent more time trying to figure out how to mitigate against those issues.

I geared each event I did in that year toward practicing the mental strengthening techniques I was learning. I completely aimed my training toward building endurance and strength so I could cover the 314 miles unsupported. My mind was always on "what would I do at Vol State?"

Reflect on:

What is the thing you want more than anything? Make an honest assessment of how focused you are on achieving this goal.

Is this enough focus for you?

If not, what do you want to change to increase the possibility of achieving this?

Note: These life lessons are just as important when dealing with not so good life situations too. If your child has cancer and you feel you have no control over the outcome, allow yourself to feel the emotions and even express them. Find someone that can support you. Then write about what you can control and what you can't. Now focus ALL your energy on the things you can control. You can give love - that is within your control. Focus your every thought and action on and in love!

Reflections

Life Lesson

Use the "pack and mail" routine to identify and release those things in life that you cannot control. Take your worries, fears, anxieties, concerns and uncertainties out of your knapsack and put them in a package (big or little, whatever is needed), address the package to the Universe (or your higher power) or at least mail it to your home. Put it in the mailbox, close the slot and wipe your hands free of those concerns. Now they are no longer yours to carry. You have given them to someone or something else to take care of for you.

Reflect on:

Write the things you can't control but that seem to bother you.

Now practice the "pack and mail" system and repeat as often as necessary.

Reflections

Life Lesson

Make it a practice to use this technique. Use kinesthetic reinforcement while telling yourself, "I can do this". Oppose your thumb to index, long, ring and little finger as I say each word–I (thumb to index), CAN (thumb to long finger), DO (thumb to ring finger), THIS (thumb to little finger).

Reflect on:

Practice this no matter what the situation or where you are!

Reflections

Life Lesson

Create (and stick to) a morning routine. If possible, do the same with the evening. The morning routine is the best way to develop discipline. It's also a great way to get important things done first thing in the morning before other life events get in the way. Establishing an evening routine is also a good way to wind down before bed and will help you get sleep and if you plan the next day's activities (I call them my intentions), it will help you sleep better. I haven't mastered the evening routine yet, but I have done the morning routine almost every morning for over one and a half years (only missing when I'm at a race): make my bed; write key things in my journal for the day before; write in my gratitude journal; and I read 20 pages a day. As a result, I read 44 books from January 2022 to November 2022.

Reflect on:

What's one thing you make into a morning routine?

Maybe it's just making the bed.

Maybe it's meditating every day.

What is important to you?

You may have to get up a bit early to achieve these things but try to start with something that will be fairly easy.

Keep track of your progress.

Reflections

Life Lesson

Obstacles can start out being objective facts and, depending on other variables, turn into monsters. Once let out of their cage, these monsters attack every part of our being. With consistent practice, we can prevent or at least minimize this onslaught. Even when things are going well, adversity can show its head. You just have to deal with it and keep going, knowing that it will pass. Never let an adversity get you down. You can outlast it. Build your resilience and ask yourself what lessons you learned from each event. You can get through it!

Reflect on:

What are your tools and techniques for dealing with adversity and conquering obstacles?

Who can you turn to for help?

What has been your pattern in the past?

What would you like to change, if anything, regarding your handling of adversity?

Reflections

Life Lesson

Control what you can control. Then focus on that. It does no good to pay attention to or "worry" about something you have absolutely no control over. Worry energy is negative energy too. You don't want to be wasting energy. Become disciplined and stay within your narrow circle of control. You can look up Stephen Covey's circle of concern and circle of influence, which has also been adapted to include a circle of control.

Reflect on:

This might take some time. Make a list of things that concern you (threat of war, the stock market, cost of education, cost of housing, etc.).

Then make a list of things you can influence (whether people like you, what people think of you, your reputation, a promotion, your work, etc.).

Lastly, make a list of the things you can control and be careful here. You may think you can control the time you need to spend transporting your kids to different activities, but are you really in control of that? You can control the time you go to bed, what you eat, what and how much you drink, if and how much you exercise, your response to your thoughts and emotions, your mood, your work ethic, your activities (at least some of them- separate out the ones you can't control but perhaps can influence).

When you're feeling stymied or stressed, look at what you're doing or trying to do and see if, perhaps, you're worrying about or spending time on things you cannot control. You can work your butt off on a project trying to get praise from your boss) but you really don't control that. You control how much you care about the product you're producing and therefore can produce it based on that. Always stick to the things you can do something about!

Reflections

Life Lesson

No one is 'average.' That requires comparing yourself to others, and that's the quickest way to unhappiness that I know. You are unique and have so much to offer. Maybe you're ready to step beyond what you've "always" done, and that's great. It makes you different, not average.

Reflect on:

What words do you use to describe yourself? Are there qualities you'd like to develop?

What makes some other people you know unique? List the features under each name.

What makes you unique?

What about yourself makes you happy?

If there are characteristics you don't like, what steps can you take to fix that?

Reflections

Life Lesson

Age is a chronological state, not a mental state. Stop telling yourself you're too old or even that you're old. Just tell yourself you feel great and youthful and love life. Keep telling yourself that and you'll believe it and live as if it's true. The mind can do miraculous things.

Reflect on:

Remove "I'm old", "I'm getting old", "I'm too old" or any reference to your age from your vocabulary. If you have to say something, say "I'm experienced!"

Throughout the day, say:

"I have so much to offer!"

"I can mentor anyone who wants some help."

"I have what it takes to be a 'life' coach for sure."

Reflections

Life Lesson

Start planning now for the things you think you'd like to do when you stop doing what you're doing now. If you have something big happening, make sure you plan for what you're going to do when it's done. This prevents post-event let-down, which can lead to depression and despair.

Reflect on:

If you have a big goal ahead, decide now (or over the next few weeks/month) what your next big goal is going to be. Start planning it in your mind at least so it develops a firm foundation.

Once you accomplish what you're working on now, give yourself time to rest, but always keep the vision of this next goal in your mind. This should help prevent the let down depression.

Reflections

Life Lesson

Every person you touch is a part of your village. How are you treating them? How do you let them know they matter - or maybe you don't let them know that but should? Start now. List the people who've come into your life even for a short period. Then write something special about them. If you know how to get in touch with them, let them know how they affected you. If you don't, then just send your gratitude to the Universe. It knows how to reach them.

Reflect on:

Who makes up your village

What do you do for them to let them know they are such an important part of your life?

What more can you do?

Reflections

Life Lesson

Be happy now, not "when." Now is all you have, so figure out what it will take in this moment to make you smile. That's where your happiness will come from. Aim for a future goal but do everything you can to relish the journey.

Reflect on:

What do you frequently think or say? Is it something like "when I lose weight, I'll feel better and be happier" or "when we get another house, we'll be happy"?

You may not use the exact word "happy" but if you're qualifying your happiness, satisfaction, or joy, you're making a big mistake. "When" may never come.

Choose to be happy NOW.

Stop putting conditions on it.

Reflections

Life Lesson

You will get through your race and your life if you realize you don't need to attach meaning or emotion to stressors. You can make a choice. You can continue to be overwhelmed by all you have going on, or you can look at everything, pare the list down and just accept what's left. The more you dwell on the negative, the more depleted you'll be and the more overwhelmed you'll feel. Do you want to move forward in life or just keep going around in circles? Practice separating reality or objectivity from your emotional responses.

Reflect on:

When you're feeling stressed out or confused or anxious or in any way uncomfortable, stop and ask yourself "what emotions am I feeling right now?" Write them down.

Next, find some object (marbles, tennis balls, LEGO blocks, golf balls, whatever) to symbolize those emotions. Label them and keep them in an "emotions box".

When faced with a situation ("I have all these bills to pay and don't have the money")write it on a piece of paper. Get your "emotions" out of the box and cover your situation.

Now, move these balls off the paper so you can look at the situation (the words) with a clear perspective with nothing clouding the picture.

Pick up a notebook and record the things you can do to work on this situation. Don't forget that your first "solution" should almost always be "I can ask someone for help"!

The more you do this, the less you'll actually need the props. You'll be able to do it in your head, but using the props is always fun.

Reflections

Life Lesson

Ask yourself, "So what if they reject me? What proof do I have that this is even a possibility? What is it I'm really afraid of?" Answer these questions and it will help you get out of the cage that fear has you confined in.

Reflect on:

The key to most of these things is finding specific evidence. Every time you "feel" something that is negative. "I can't do anything right" should immediately lead to you a follow-up of "what evidence supports this?" Make yourself stop until you can produce the evidence. If you can't, then reframe the sentence.

How can you use THIS particular thing as feedback and as a means for change?

Is there proof that most of the time you do things right?

Make the "Fact Checker" your favorite companion.

Reflections

Life Lesson

The part of you that's worried that people will laugh at you is young and scared. It's trying to keep you from doing anything that in the past would have caused other kids or adults to ridicule you. 99% of the time people won't laugh at you. They probably have had the same fears and if you share that fear, they might help you overcome it.

Reflect on:

What are not doing because you are afraid that people will laugh at you or make fun of you?

Another place to bring in the "Fact Checker".

In what situations have people actually made fun of you or laughed at you? When was that? How old were you? What's different right now?

Write these discussions out so you can see them in black and white. Reassure your brain that you may have been afraid of that when you were a child, but now you're grown up and the likelihood it will happen is small to zero.

Reflections

Life Lesson

Fatigue is a like a wheel with all the spokes representing different factors. It's so important to attend to the variety of factors that compound not only your level of fatigue, but your perception of it. You must stay ahead of the fatigue you can control (e.g., proper fueling and hydration, emotional baggage, mental requirements) so that you can deal with any fatigue you can't control (emergencies, jobs, etc.).

Reflect on:

Think back to a time when you felt significant fatigue.

What was going on in your life then? Were there physical illnesses involved? Were there big stresses in your life?

What did you do to resolve the fatigue?

In the future (or even in the present) what can you do to help yourself when you feel fatigued? Make a list of physical aspects, emotional concerns and thought (mental) issues.

Are you training for something hard and are worn out physically? Did you just start exercising and maybe you've overdone it?

Are you dealing with other stresses in your life - at work, family, financial, education, etc.?

How much sleep are you getting and what's its quality?

What are your most common thoughts? Are you worrying? Are you a catastrophizer? Or are you just trying to barge through the fatigue without attending to it? None of these options is healthy. What can you do to change your relationship with your body and your fatigue?

Reflections

Life Lesson

An issue can remain foremost in your mind, but it doesn't have to bring along the attendant fear. We attach emotions to events/situations. We don't have to do that. Fear only releases chemicals that negatively affect your performance and don't help solve the problem. Keep the issue and the fear about the issue separate. This takes much practice and may be a place where some sort of mantra would be helpful.

Reflect on:

What are the issues on your mind right now?

What fears come up when you think about this issue?

Is each fear realistic?

What do you feel in your body when you have that fear?

Is there anxiety? Do you shake?

Create a mantra to counter this fear whenever its ugly head rears itself. Then use it.

Reflections

Life Lesson

A road race is a metaphor for how we run our lives and how we compete against the various forces and foes we feel we're up against all the time in life. Your biggest opponent and the one you must learn to tackle first is yourself.

Reflect on:

How have you gotten in your own way in the past? Identify the specifics if you can. Can you laugh at this?

Visualize yourself shadow boxing with yourself and see the self that gets in the way shrinking, getting smaller and smaller.

Eventually, in your mind movie, you'll be declared the victor because the shadow you is now out of the way. See the referee raising your hand in the air, proclaiming you champion! How do you feel now?

Reflections

Life Lesson

No matter where you go in life, you're going to run into obstacles. It's your choice, though, whether you let them stop you and make you turn around or whether you simply decide to find a way around them. Train yourself to pick the "I can conquer this" route and mentality, and you'll be a success in life. Find a way over those boulders!

Reflect on:

What obstacles are you facing right now?

Have they slowed you down?

What can you say to them to let them know you won't let them rule your life?

Reflections

Life Lesson

The burdens on your back are mostly old hurts and resentments mixed in with worries about the future "what ifs." Take some time and evaluate this weight and see what you can offload. It will make your life so much easier and so much more fun! Even though it takes time and is difficult, de-cluttering your heart, mind and soul will lighten your life and increase your joy. Some "emergency" stuff is good, but for most people it's just fear driving the need for each item. Try your best to release that fear and see what you can really get along with and without. Your pack may seem light... until it isn't. Constantly examine the contents and see what you can eliminate and in what areas others might assist you. Ask yourself if your ultimate health is worth swallowing your pride and asking for help. Anything is worth more than getting sick, quitting, or having a breakdown. I know; it happened to me.

Reflect on:

What burdens are you carrying right now? List them all.

Did any of these worsen the burden?

Past hurts, Resentments, or Worries about the future?

For each of the above, ask yourself (and write it down) what you think you can do about it. For example, you can't do squat to change the past; the resentments you hold are only doing harm to you, not the person or thing you resent. What control do you have over the "worries"?

Remember, focus on the things you can control.

What can you release? What are you WILLING to release?

Reflections

Life Lesson

More on burdens. Most of these burdens that we hold on to are simply limiting beliefs or ideas we've absorbed from others who repeated them endlessly as we were growing up. If you search for proof that you really are as bad as you think and do so objectively, you'll surprise yourself when you find out that you don't have any valid proof and these things you're thinking about yourself are not true.

Reflect on:

What are your beliefs about yourself? Put down both good and bad.

Now, for the negative ones, write about where they came from. Maybe from your parents, teachers, peers, siblings or religious leaders. Think hard because these beliefs began a very long time ago.

For each belief, starting with the limiting or negative ones, document the EVIDENCE, supporting that this belief is true.

If you can't find objective evidence, ask yourself if they really are true.

Can you release them?

Reflections

Life Lesson

Make an outline of your life. This should include where you are now, where you came from, what tools you've accumulated, what internal factors are you dealing with (e.g., lack of confidence, insecurity, anger, depression, etc.), what external factors are involved (personal illness, illness of a family member, career changes, relationship issues, financial problems, etc.). Then figure out what you need to deal with daily and how well equipped you are to deal with all of it. Make a list of resources. Then make a plan. One of the most important steps is to take the time to decide what really needs to be on the list. Often, we are so overwhelmed that it isn't until we put things out of our brain and onto paper that we see so much extraneous stuff that we can eliminate.

Reflect on:

Start this outline of your life. If you're creative, maybe you can make a drawing or a group of circles.

In one column (or circle) put all the goals you've made.

Column/circle 2 should contain a list of all your accomplishments.

The third section is for the tools/techniques you've accumulated and used (e.g., therapy, IFS, meditation, EFT, acupuncture, massage, journaling, etc.)

What are the internal factors in your life (e.g. fear, anxiety, insecurity, uncertainty, etc.)? This goes in section 4.

Next, list the external factors (illness - yourself or of a family, finances, relationship issues, etc.).

How well equipped to deal with daily stress do you think you are?
What did reviewing your life show you?

Reflections

Life Lesson

Make a "Magic Memory Box". Memories and stories help carry you through tough times, especially when you dedicate yourself to that person's memory. When life seems tough and you're facing some sort of adversity, stop and ask yourself, "Is this really that bad"? Then think about someone who's going through something so terrible you're glad it's not your burden. Find someone or some situation to think about when you're sending out invites to your personal pity party! Change your perspective after that. Be happy and know that you are meant to experience the obstacle and conquer the challenge. It will strengthen you for whatever else is coming into your life.

Reflect on:

You can use a cookie jar approach to this too. On a piece of paper, write things that bring joy and happiness to you when you think about them. Put the slips of paper in a jar. Make a label for it and put it in a sacred place.

Whenever you're feeling down or doubtful about your ability to handle something, pull out a "Magic memory" and recreate the experience in your mind.

Eventually, you will commit them all to your mind, and you can call them up at will.

Reflections

Reflections

Life Lesson

Rarely should you take the initial response to "Are you okay?" as the gospel truth. Most people will hide what they are really experiencing because they don't want to appear weak or don't want to bother other people. They may really need your help. Your kindness and reaching out might actually help them decide that life is still worth living. That happens more than you know.

Reflect on:

Who, in your life, are you concerned with because they just haven't seemed "themselves" lately?

What can you do to find out if you can help?

What can you do to just show someone you're there if they want/need it without feeling too pushy?

Keep track of the people around you and follow-up on their answers when appropriate. If one of your colleagues told you their kid was home from school ill, make sure you ask every day how they are doing (both the kid and the adult) until you are sure they are ok. Don't forget to ask if there is anything you can do for them.

Reflections

Life Lesson

View the unknown as just what it is - a circumstance that has components and will have a solution once you unveil those components. Refrain from seeing a green-eyed monster waiting for you behind a curtain, ready to pounce out at you. Remember what Dorothy and the others saw when Toto pulled back the curtain and exposed the real Wizard of Oz? They had made this small man into a monster the size of Goliath and with the power of God. That only keeps you in fight-or-flight mode, which will deplete your energy in ways you can't even imagine.

Reflect on:

What are the unknowns in your life right now?

Are there parts of the situation, though, that you can define? If so, focus on them and see what options are available to find a solution to them.

When you think of the "unknown" and "uncertain" aspects, visualize Dorothy and the others pulling back the curtain on the tiny little Oz trying to sound like a big, blustery badass.

Reflections

Life Lesson

Turn frustrations into learning opportunities so that you deplete no more energy than necessary, and you don't get paralyzed by not knowing what to do and you can keep moving. Don't let frustration spin into fear or anger. Step back, look at what the problem is and then go through a problem-solving technique that you use every day in life. You may not know that you do it every day, but you do. Something as simple as being stuck in traffic and you ask yourself if you should go a different route or can you listen to more of an audio book? There's a lot that goes into that decision and that's a problem-solving technique you use without even realizing it. Many of our apparent frustrations are just wrapping paper on other underlying emotions.

Reflect on:

What is your normal problem-solving system?

What keeps you from using that when you're stressed or upset?

How can you pull yourself back from the emotions and fears so that you can simply analyze the problem? Remember the discussions on chunking it down?

Reflections

Life Lesson

Sometimes, to get what you want, you have to create your own training plan. There may be no pre-made plan. When you create your own, make it as simple, realistic, and as measurable as you can. That way, you will have objective ways to determine if you're succeeding or if you need to revise the plan. This applies to life and races. Often the most successful people haven't followed "the book" but have developed creative-and effective-alternatives.

Reflect on:

Pick something simple that you want but can't immediately have for whatever reason.

What is a simple plan to help you get this thing? Maybe it's saving $10 a week for x number of weeks. Make it simple to start with and then you can do the same with bigger goals. Prove to yourself that you can do it. If saving $10 doesn't seem like something you can do, how about a dollar or five dollars? Pick something that will make you feel successful.

Do it. Act on all these things.

Reflections

Life Lesson

Find objective metrics to measure your physical progress. Never evaluate it based on how you feel. That is not accurate. If feeling is all you use, then you'll never be able to gauge what you need to do next.

Reflect on:

What is your physical goal?

How are you going to reach it? What's your plan? If you're going to build muscle, what will be the metrics will used to know it's working? If you don't have the metrics (and don't use them) you'll never know whether your plan is working. What good is it then? You can't just "think" you're stronger.

Same goes with weight. Maybe you'll feel lighter, but what does the scale say? But be careful not to get weighed every day and expect to have lost 10 pounds in two days.

You're running or riding a race, do the same.

Metrics and measurements define progress.

Reflections

Life Lesson

Mental training is something few people concentrate on in life. They go to the gym to build up their physical muscles, but where's the "gym" to build up their mental toughness? You really need to go to both gyms to lead a happier and more fulfilled life.

Reflect on:

What mental training do you routinely do?

Where can you go to find more about doing mental training?

Are you going to do it?

Study mental discipline and conditioning just like you regularly go to the gym.

Reflections

Life Lesson

We all take the ferry as we transition to other stages of our life whether it be sports, family, career, religion, etc. Use that time, no matter how short, to your advantage and take an inventory of where you're coming from. It's a good time to write your current values, life principles, ideals, and beliefs, as well as your assessment of your character. Write this down and then, when the race is over (the new period you've entered), re-assess everything and see if there are differences. I imagine there will be quite a few and, hopefully, it will be good and reflect major growth! Re-evaluate no matter what you do.

Remember, too, that no matter how many times you do something, it's always best to have some sort of checklist and then, of course, it only does you good if you use it. Those things you miss will surprise you if you don't use it or don't make it out far enough.

Reflect on:

If you're in some type of transition period now, no matter how big or small, take some time to inventory your successes, your perceived failures (remember, though, that they are just feedback), your beliefs and values.

Where do you want to go from here?

After this?

Reflections

Life Lesson

Always attempt to get outside of yourself and recognize those who are sacrificing so much to enable you to enjoy what you're doing. Go from "ME" to "WE" to "THEM" and you'll find so much more to be grateful for!

Reflect on:

How can you go from ME to WE in your:

Family

Friends

Work

Clubs

Religious affiliation

etc.

Reflections

Life Lesson

You never accomplish great things without the help of others. Where there is an obvious front person who has helped you get there, always look past that person to find the true stalwart force behind them.

Reflect on:

Who are those who have helped you get where you are now? Go way back and even start with your parents (if applicable)?

Any special teachers?

Friends?

People you admire but perhaps don't know?

Often our mentors are great names in history.

Reflections

Life Lesson

There's probably going to be someone bigger than life in your way when you're after a goal that's huge. Just remember that David was NOT the odds-on favorite to beat Goliath, but he did. If you tackle each adversity you meet with the same determination and perseverance, you will succeed just like David did.

Reflect on:

Who or what is your Goliath?

Are you going to be like David or just roll over?

What's your metaphorical slingshot?

Reflections

Life Lesson

The width of the shoulder (ability to carry your load) and terrain (perhaps some rumble strips which symbolize those constant bumps in your way whether they are physical, mental or emotional) are probably the most significant factors in how you survive each day or progress toward each goal you have. It pays to develop the proper tactics to deal with every type of shoulder.

Reflect on:

How do you assess your ability to carry the load upon your shoulders?

Could it be improved? If so, how?

What are your personal "rumble strips"? Physical, emotional, and mental?

Reflections

Life Lesson

Rumble strips have meaning in your life. What difficulties have you had to navigate and how has your problem-solving benefited you? What wake-up calls have you received? And which ones have you answered? Our job is to look for the opportunity to grow from encountering those nasty little grooves in the road!

Reflect on:

Take some time to list the difficulties you've come across in your life.

Write enough about them so that you fully remember what you went through and what you did to overcome them.

What problem-solving techniques have you learned work for you?

Have you had any wake-up calls? List them if you have.

Reflections

Life Lesson

A guardrail will always show up when you most need it. You can make it until then. When you find your friend, the guardrail, cherish it, talk with it, love it and then vow to model it for others you'll meet on your life's path. Be to others what that guardrail was to you - a beacon of hope and love.

Reflect on:

What have been your guardrails (places you can lean on and rest at. They help you take the load off for a bit)? Think of things or people that have shown up just when you needed them... perhaps a book or a special friend.

Reflections

Life Lesson

Roads have varying degrees of reflectivity, as does life. When your path seems darkest, slow down if you must, but always keep going. You will either reach another well-reflected road with street lamps shining down on you or daylight will dawn. Just keep going and learn from the darkness. If you absolutely must, you can pull over and regroup/rest until the sun rises once again in your life.

Reflect on:

Think back to when your life seemed darkest. Was there any glimmer of light in the distance?

Did you first react? If so, how?

Did you simply respond? If so, what made you able to stay rational enough to place response over reaction?

What did you do to get through it?

What helped you?

Reflections

Life Lesson

Try this exercise with your life. List all the pertinent waypoints along your journey and add a little tidbit about them. Your life is a series of travels from one place to another. That travelogue tells a better story than you could ever see in the movies.

Reflect on:

This is like another reflection, but less complicated. I found it fun and intriguing.

List the important way points in your life, adding a bit about each. Be creative.

Is there any pattern you can see there?

Reflections

Life Lesson

You should have a "file cabinet" of your experiences. You can then search through this list of files whenever you come across what appears to be a new situation or something you don't know how to handle. You can do this on paper and then install the info in your brain. Doing it on paper (or computer) helps you recognize that you have plenty of skills and experiences from which to gain ideas. Always be updating the files in your file cabinet. Each experience adds something new - or maybe even lets you know that there is a file that needs to be deleted. You can consider almost anything a data bit in your file cabinet. Something you've read, something someone else has given or told you about, or something you've experienced already. Maybe even something about an experience that seems totally unrelated. It may hold the one clue that helps you piece it all together.

Reflect on:

Start recording your personal file cabinet so you get into the habit.

You don't have to do this for everything if you don't want to.

But if you recognize you've "come across something like this" before, it will help calm you and soothe your brain. Then you can apply this info to the current situation.

Reflections

Life Lesson

No matter what happens in your life, Find a Way! Whenever things seem impossible, tell yourself you will find a way. You will ask someone for help! There is a way out there.

Reflect on:

How will you find a way when you need it?

Reflections

About the Author:

Dr. Terrie Wurzbacher served as a U.S. Navy physician for more than 29 years during which she cultivated a passion for endurance running and walking. Overcoming multiple challenges in her seven decades, she has an exceptional understanding of techniques and attitudes that can help you avoid and overcome the stumbling blocks to smooth sailing.

Terrie outlined her journey to conquer the 314 mile race across Tennessee (the Last Annual Volunteer State 500k) in her book *It's Not About the Miles: Lessons from the Road*, available on Amazon.

Keep up with Terrie's latest ventures at her blog at TerrieWurzbacher.com